Make Your Own Art

Card Making

FRANKLIN WATTS
LONDON•SYDNEY

First published in 2008 by Franklin Watts

© 2008 Arcturus Publishing Limited

Franklin Watts
338 Euston Road
London NW1 3BH

Franklin Watts Australia
Level 17/207 Kent Street, Sydney, NSW 2000

Produced by Arcturus Publishing Limited,
26/27 Bickels Yard, 151–153 Bermondsey Street,
London SE1 3HA

Editor: Alex Woolf
Designers: Sally Henry and Trevor Cook
Consultant: Daisy Fearns

Picture credits: Sally Henry and Trevor Cook

Every attempt has been made to clear copyright.
Should there be any inadvertent omission,
please apply to the publisher for rectification.

A CIP catalogue record for this book is available
from the British Library.

Dewey Decimal Classification Number: 745.594'1

ISBN 978 0 7496 8187 6

Printed in China

Franklin Watts is a division of Hachette Children's Books,
an Hachette Livre UK company
www.hachettelivre.co.uk

Contents

Introduction

Greetings cards

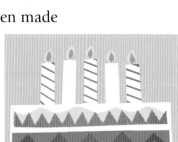

A greetings card is always more welcome when it has been made by the person sending it. In this book you'll find lots of ways to make your cards even more special.

4

Paper and card

You need a supply of coloured paper and card.

Paper: All sizes are useful, but you may need larger pieces to make special, oversize envelopes.

Card: It's important that your card will stand up and keep its shape. Larger cards have to be made from thicker card.

Folding and cutting

In our instructions, we use a dotted line to show a **fold** and a solid line for a **cut**. There's usually a fold or an edge that the folded part has to meet.

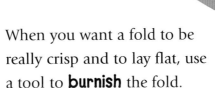

fold line

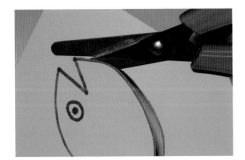

cutting along a line

When you want a fold to be really crisp and to lay flat, use a tool to **burnish** the fold.

Safety first

Always ask an adult to help you when you are using sharp objects, such as scissors or thumbtacks.

burnishing a fold

Glue

glue stick

There are three sorts of glue you may need. The sort that comes as a **glue stick** is ideal for sticking card and paper. Place the piece to be glued face down on a clean scrap paper and apply the glue evenly, working from the middle towards the edge. Spread the glue right onto the scrap paper. There shouldn't be any excess or blobs on the front.

White craft glue will stick paper and card well, but tends to distort if spread over a large area. It's good for drawing with glitter (see page 27).

Universal glue comes in a tube and is best for sticking odd-shaped things or unusual materials. It won't distort card if used correctly, but can 'string' so test it on scrap first.

rubber cement

white craft glue

Presentation

It's great to be able to give your friends a beautiful, unusual or funny greetings card that you've made yourself. We've got lots of designs to choose from. There are shaped and three-dimensional as well as conventional ones. You can use paint, pens or collage to make your cards.

Design

All the designs in this book are based on something that will fold up and fit into an envelope. It's very important that your finished card will fit, so it's a good idea to have the envelope ready when you start work.

Standard envelopes

For most projects an ordinary envelope will do for your card. You can get coloured ones from craft shops. They are often made in unusual shapes, so shop around. If you want a particular size and you can't find it, you can make your own using the simple guide opposite.

Make your own envelopes

In the picture we've shown the shape of the finished paper (orange) you will need to make the envelope (red). You can adapt this design to different shapes of envelope. Ask an adult to help you with cutting out the diamond shape. Make sure you cut the curved parts exactly as shown.

Finish the envelope as follows:

- Fold the bottom flap up.
- Fold the side flaps, glue their lower edges and stick down to the bottom flap.
- Fold the top flap down.

Don't stick the top flap down until you have put your card inside!

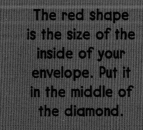

a

trip of glue

The red shape is the size of the inside of your envelope. Put it in the middle of the diamond.

c

d

b

Distance a to b is twice the height of the red shape plus 25mm (1in). Distance c to d is twice the width of the red shape plus 25mm (1in).

Birthday cake

Celebrate a special birthday with this cake and candles card.

You will need:

- Coloured paper
- Thin white card
- Corrugated paper
- Scissors, glue stick
- Large envelope

35 MINUTES

What to do...

Fold your white card into a tent shape. Use more white card for the candles. Choose brightly coloured papers to make the cut-out shapes.

5 MINUTES

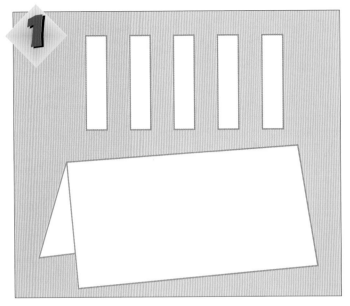

Cut out thin strips of white card for the candles. Make as many as you need.

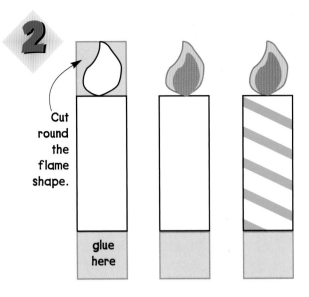

Cut out a flame shape at the top of each candle. Stick on the coloured paper flames and stripes.

Cut round the flame shape.

glue here

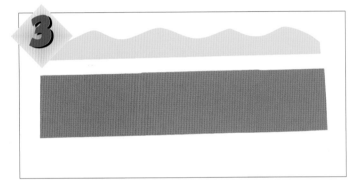

Cut an oblong shape for the cake band and a wavy shape for the marzipan. Glue them on.

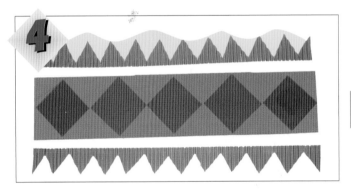

Cut some zigzag strips and diamond shapes and stick them in position (see opposite page).

Glue the candles to the back of the card. Space them out evenly. The card is complete!

Write your greeting inside the card. If you need to make an special envelope, see page 7.

9

Tortoise and hare

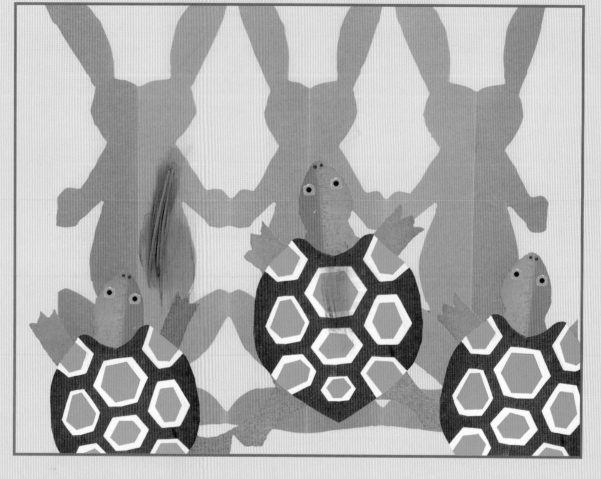

Making this design is very quick, but make sure you follow the cutting instructions carefully! We've made hares and tortoises, but you can try any animals to make your cards.

You will need:

- Coloured papers
- Scissors
- Glue stick
- Pencil and markers
- Envelopes

20 MINUTES

What to do...

Always make sharp accurate folds in your paper. Cut as neatly as you can to give smooth edges to your cards. Always make sure you're not cutting the joining parts on the fold!

5 MINUTES

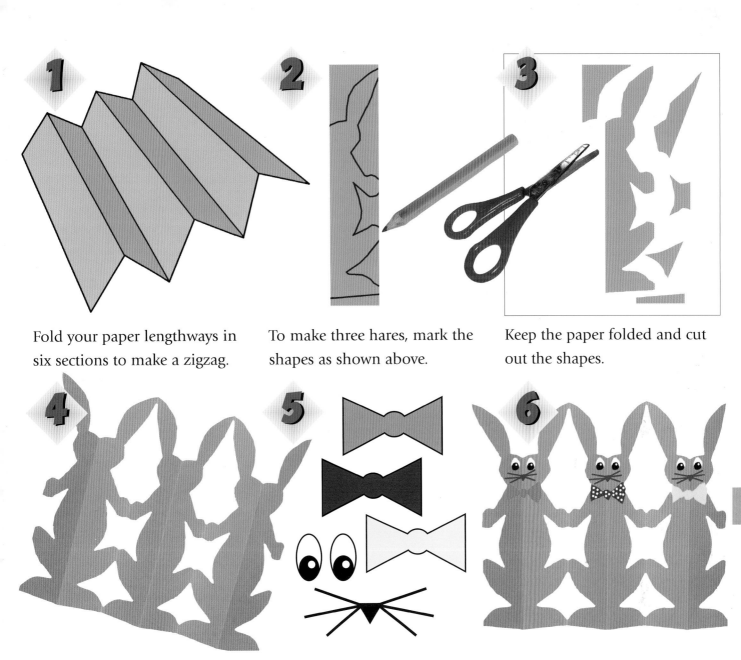

1 Fold your paper lengthways in six sections to make a zigzag.

2 To make three hares, mark the shapes as shown above.

3 Keep the paper folded and cut out the shapes.

4 Open your card out. Now we need some details.

5 Cut out three bow-ties in different colours.

6 Stick them on. Cut out and glue on noses, eyes and whiskers.

1 Repeat the method. This time we're making tortoises!

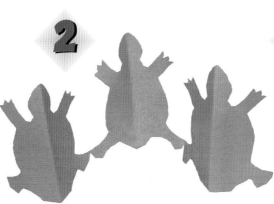

2 Mark the shapes with a pencil. Cut out with scissors and open.

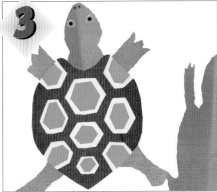

3 Decorate the shells. Don't forget the greetings on the back!

Stamp designs

35 MINUTES

5 MINUTES

Stamped designs are simple but quick and fun to make. You can change your stamps to suit the occasion or the person the card is for.

You will need:

- *Coloured card, envelopes*
- *Sponge kitchen cloth*
- *Plastic lids from aerosols*
- *Scissors, universal glue*
- *Marker pens*
- *Paint brush*
- *Poster paints*
- *Tissues to clean up*

What to do...

Draw some simple outlines on paper or directly onto some sponge cloth. Our card has frogs, water lilies and ducks. Copy the templates on the opposite page or you can draw your own designs. Make sure your image will fit on the flat side of your aerosol lid. After you have finished, wash your stamps under the tap and keep them for next time.

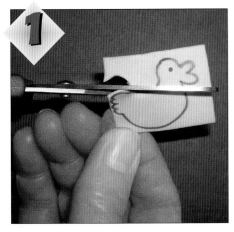

Draw shapes on sponge cloth and cut them out.

You can use paper patterns if you find this easier.

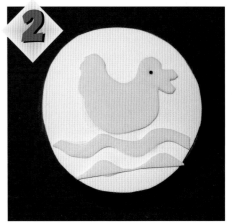

Stick the shapes onto a plastic lid and allow the glue to dry.

Use thick poster paint to cover the raised part of your stamp.

Turn the lid over and press the stamp on to the card.

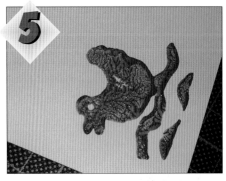

Lift off to reveal the first image. Repeat from step 3.

13

Work from left to right so that you don't smudge your work (or right to left if you are left-handed). Let the paint dry.

Make up more stamps to finish your card.

You can use half a potato to make a stamp. Carefully cut patterns on the flat side. Ask an adult to help.

Button badges

Your friends will be
delighted if you give
them badges. Create
unusual card badges
with safety pins.
It's easy!
Just follow
steps 1 to 4.

You will need:

- *Thin card, needle and cotton*
- *Coloured felt, coloured paper*
- *Buttons, safety pins, pencil*
- *Scissors, envelopes*

25 MINUTES

What to do...

Sort out your materials into
sets of three colours that go
well together.

5 MINUTES

1 Draw and cut out some flower shapes in different coloured felt or similar material.

2 Try different shapes and colours together. Use curves, zigzags and fringes.

3 Choose a coloured button for each badge. Sew the button on with a needle and cotton to keep all the shapes together.

4 Sew a safety pin to the back of each badge. Pin the badges to folded cards. Use them for your party invitations or just for fun!

15

more ideas for badges, with two buttons

Birthday clowns

45 MINUTES

5 MINUTES

16

You will need:

- *Coloured card, a large envelope*
- *Scissors, glue stick, a drawing pin*
- *Markers and a pencil*
- *5 paper fasteners, string, glitter*
- *Plastic wobbly eyes (optional)*

What to do...

Copy or trace the shapes opposite onto coloured card, then cut them out. Decorate the shapes with stuck-on coloured paper or draw in the details with marker pens. Check that the complete card fits the envelope.

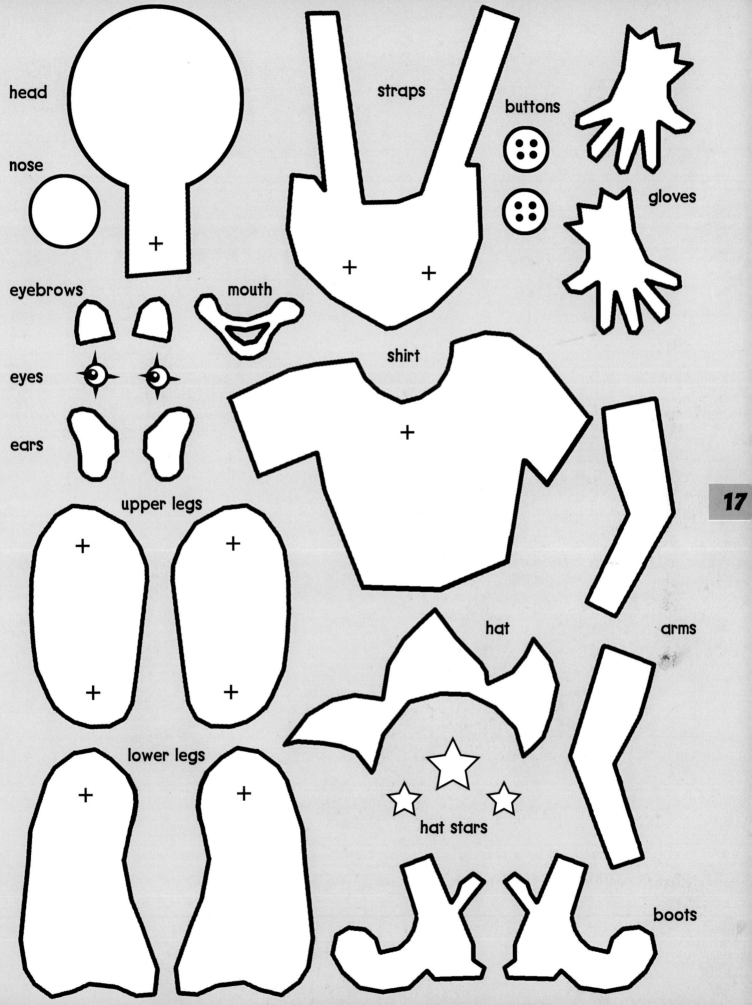

head

nose

straps

buttons

gloves

eyebrows

mouth

eyes

shirt

ears

upper legs

17

hat

arms

lower legs

hat stars

boots

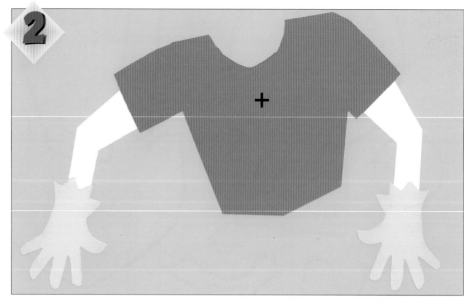

Find his head shape and stick his hat on. Glue on his nose, eyebrows, eyes and mouth. Stick on his ears, then put the stars on his hat!

Find his arms, two gloves and shirt. Stick his arms behind his shirt and his gloves over his arms as shown. Glue the straps over his shirt. Stick on both the buttons. Allow it to dry.

You will see crosses (+) on the template shapes. These show where you should make a small hole with a drawing pin. The holes are for paper fasteners.

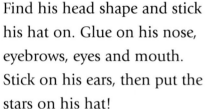

Paper fastener

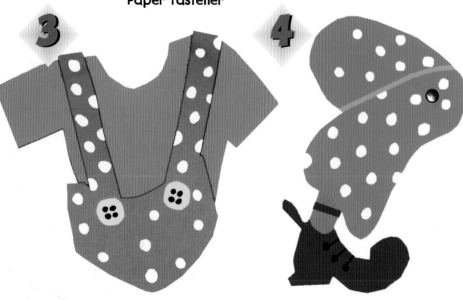

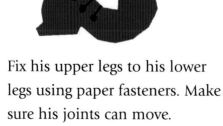

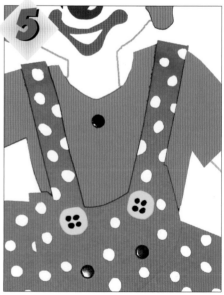

Stick his boots to the lower halves of the trousers and point them left and right!

Fix his upper legs to his lower legs using paper fasteners. Make sure his joints can move.

With more fasteners, join his legs to his body, then fix his head to his shirt. Add a string loop to his hat.

Check you haven't left any pieces out. Write a greeting on the back of your clown. Swing his arms and legs round to fit in a big envelope (see page 7) and address it to your friend.

19

Fairy

Robot

Pirate

Here are some other faces to copy if you want to make more fun birthday cards. They will also make great party invitations. Write all the details about the party on the back of the cards. Invent some exciting new clothes for these people to wear. Make templates to check how the pieces go together. Glue and fasten as before. Add some glitter for sparkle. Enjoy the party!

Pop-up greetings

This pop-up card can be adapted for many occasions. We made a frog, but you can easily make an Easter chick or an octopus – they both have a beak!

You will need:

- *Cartridge paper*
- *Coloured marker pens*
- *Scissors, pencil, ruler*
- *Envelope*

25
MINUTES

What to do...

Fold a piece of thick paper, 410 x 230mm (16 x 9in) in half, then in half again.

2
MINUTES

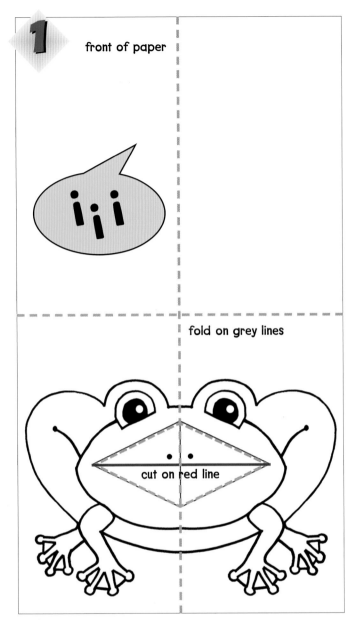

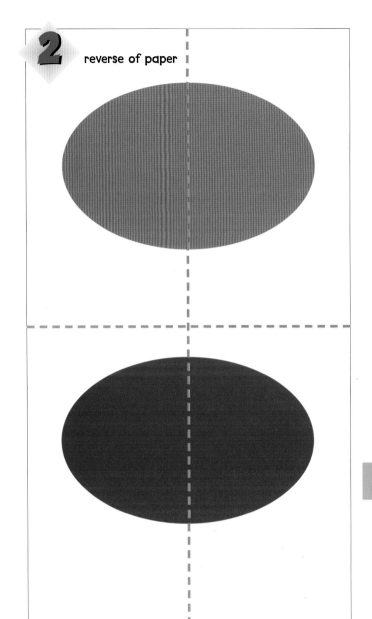

21

Draw and colour the frog. The mouth should be 125mm (5in) long and go across the middle of the card. Draw the diamond-shape fold lines. Open the page up and score these lines. Fold back along the long fold and cut the mouth line with scissors. Fold along the dotted lines for the upper and lower part of the frog's mouth. Open it out again, turn it over and paint the patches of colour for the inside of the mouth and allow it to dry. Fold the card again, this time making sure the mouth parts stick out so that the card closes with the mouth wide open.

Write your message in a speech bubble on the front.

Paper weaving

Happy Birthday

Best Wishes

Can you find a picture in a magazine that you'd really like for a greetings card? Here is a great way to give it the wow factor!

You will need:

- *Thin card, white or coloured*
- *Marker pens, pencil, ruler*
- *Coloured magazine pictures*
- *Black and white photocopies*
- *Scissors, glue stick*
- *Envelopes*

25 MINUTES

What to do...

Choose a colour picture you like. Find one with a clear image or pattern. Complicated pictures don't work so well.

5 MINUTES

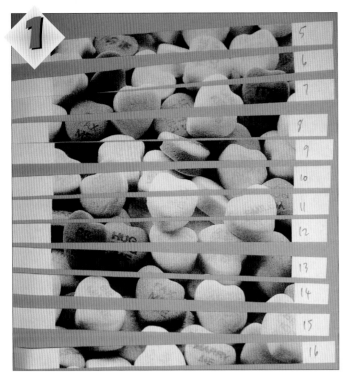

Trim the card to fit your envelope. Get a photocopy of your picture. Cut the copy side to side in 12mm (0.5in) strips. Number the strips.

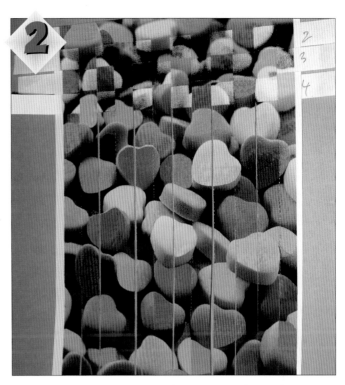

Make cuts 12mm (0.5in) apart in the colour picture, but leave the top 12mm (0.5in) attached. Stick the top edge down.

Start weaving the strips of the copy over and under the colour picture, starting at the top.

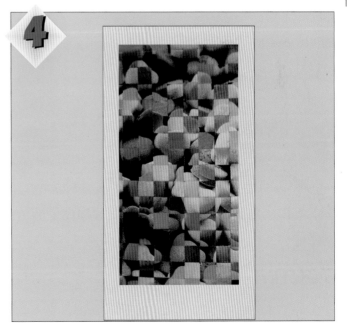

Continue to weave the whole picture. Use the numbers to check the strips are in the right order. Now just add your greeting.

Opposites

15
MINUTES

2
MINUTES

Opposites – a really quick and effective way to make cards!
Keep to simple shapes and have fun.

You will need:

- *Coloured paper*
- *Thin white card, pencil*
- *Scissors, glue stick*
- *Envelopes*

What to do...

Think of a simple design for your card, or copy ours. Notice that you only need to draw half of the shape. First, fold your white card and trim it to fit your envelope. We found a square envelope for our card, but you can adapt your design to suit the shape of your envelope.

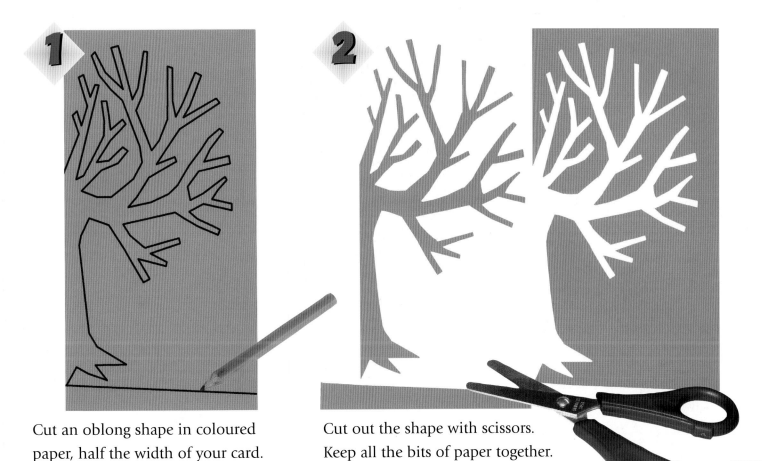

1 Cut an oblong shape in coloured paper, half the width of your card. Draw half the shape in pencil.

2 Cut out the shape with scissors. Keep all the bits of paper together.

25

3

Glue a different colour paper on your folded card as a background, leaving a narrow white edge. Stick down the right-hand side of your tree first, keeping it straight. Turn the cut-out shapes over and fit them together. Glue them in place. Put your personal message on the inside!

Try other designs using four sides.

Glitter and glue

Exchanging cards is traditional at certain times of the year, especially at Christmas. By making drawings in glue and adding glitter you can make your designs sparkle!

You will need:

- Coloured paper or card
- Marker pens, scissors
- White craft glue
- Coloured glitter
- Envelopes

35 MINUTES

What to do...

Fold and trim your cards to fit your envelopes. For Christmas you could find a real holly leaf to copy. For Halloween we have drawn a pumpkin with a face.

10 MINUTES

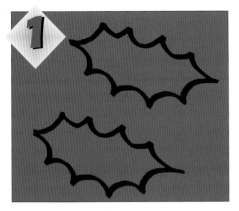

Draw two holly leaf shapes on some green paper.

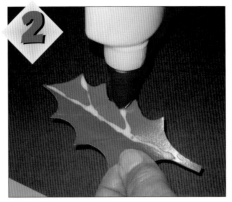

Cut the leaves out and use glue to draw in the veins.

Sprinkle glitter onto the wet glue and shake off the excess.

Stick the leaves on the card. Now put some glue and red glitter for berries!

Always allow the glue to dry completely before putting your card in the envelope!

More ideas for cards

- Snowman
- Snow crystals
- Christmas pudding
- Presents in a stocking
- Christmas cracker
- Easter Bunny
- Get Well Soon!
- Valentine Hearts

Draw a pencil guide line or use glue directly on your card to make an outline of a pumpkin. Add the glitter and tip off the excess. Put in glue triangles for eyes and nose. Draw the teeth.

Shake on some more glitter. Let the glue dry. It's finished!

Write greetings inside for your friends. They'll love the cards.

Hints and Tips: Work on a big sheet of paper so that you can collect all the dropped glitter for next time!

Pirates ahoy!

Make this unusual card on a pirate theme. It's a complete adventure story in a card!

You will need:

- Coloured papers, thin card
- Coloured marker pens
- Fine black marker pen
- Scissors, paper glue stick
- Large envelope

35 MINUTES

What to do...

A4 size card is ideal for this project. Fold it in half, short side to short side, then fold it again and again making a zigzag so you have eight sides.

5 MINUTES

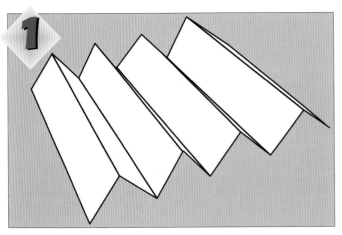

Look at the templates on page 30. Start with the sea at the bottom of the page. Trace or copy the shape onto blue paper. Cut along the wavy line to make two sets of waves.

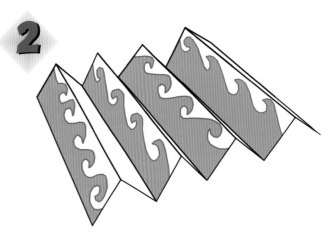

Repeat this for four sets. Trim the sides to fit the card. The tops of the waves should be just below the folds. Stick them on the first, third, fifth and seventh faces of your zigzag card.

Choose the pirate captain from the templates. Cut him out in card and add coloured paper for his clothes, or colour him in with markers. Draw the details with a fine black marker pen. Glue the tab shown in yellow on the template..

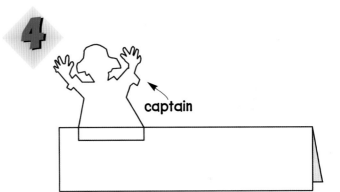

Attach it to the back of the first zigzag. Glue the captain on the back of the first wave. Glue the other cut-outs in place. The mate doesn't have a tab. Stick him on the front of the first wave.

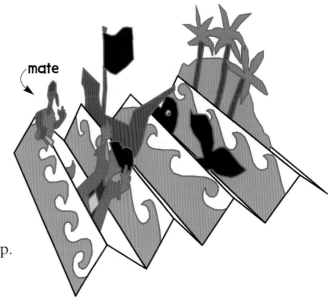

Adjust your card as shown, so that the zigzag stands up. Fold it up to go in the envelope!

island

mate

whale's tail

palm trees

pirate ship

whale

waves

shark's fin

captain

30

Glossary

Burnish   To smooth down a fold in paper with a tool – you can use a spoon or a ruler.

Card   Like paper but thicker. It must be stiff enough for the card to stand up properly.

Cartridge paper   A thick, rough-textured paper used for drawing.

Corrugated paper   A special kind of paper made from two layers of paper with a wavy layer of paper glued between them. It can be bought in art and craft shops.

Crease   A crease is the mark left by folding card or paper and flattening it out again.

Crêpe paper   This is a special sort of craft paper made with lots of little wrinkles in it. You can pull it into curved shapes like flower petals.

Diagonal   A diagonal is a line that joins the corners of a square or rectangle.

Felt   A thick soft cloth you can cut into shapes. It doesn't fray.

Oblong   An oblong is a shape like a square, but longer one way than the other.

Paper fastener   A small, two-pronged, metal item used for fixing papers together.

Parallel   Lines the same distance apart (like railway tracks) are parallel.

Pop-up   A style of card where a part of the card stands out from the fold.

Rectangle   It's the same as an oblong.

Safety pin   A pin bent round so that the point is guarded when closed.

Set square   A guide you use to make sure angles are 90°.

Paper fastener

Sponge cloth   A soft fabric, either plain or textured, available in small squares for kitchen dishcloths.

Stamp   A way of pressing a design onto paper using a pattern covered with paint.

Tab   A small flap of material attached to something.

Template   Sometimes called a pattern, a template is a guide for making lots of things the same shape. There are some on the opposite page!

Tracing paper   Thin but strong paper you can see through. Put it on top of something you want to copy, and draw on it.

Index

32